From Conflict to Collaboration: Successful Co-Parenting Ethics

By Judith F. Davis

Table Of Contents

Chapter 1: Co-Parenting And All It Entails

After a divorce, many parts of parenting stay the same. However, maintaining good parent-child communication frequently calls for much more consideration and care. Children can be particularly exposed to the emotional turmoil of divorce.

Children's lives may become even more unstable if communication between co-parents frequently involves disagreement.

Co-parents can still be a source of stability and comfort for their children even though separation will alter how families function as long as they make a positive commitment to their shared parenting.

Co-Parenting Relationship Management

If you and your spouse just got divorced, you might be unsure of where to concentrate your efforts to maintain healthy and effective family communication.

Making a start can be difficult and sometimes prevents parents who are new to co-parenting from moving forward.

Here are a few areas that will need your diligence to inspire confident co-parenting to get you started.

Make a plan and follow it

The time you invest in creating a thorough parenting plan will be worthwhile. Establishing boundaries, best practices, and expectations with your co-parent should take some time. By doing this, you will remove much of the uncertainty from your co-parenting.

A comprehensive parenting plan should specify things like how to manage requests for parenting time alterations, how to define exchange processes, and how you will communicate.

More than simply parent-child communication benefits from consistency. Children will adapt to living in two houses more easily if there is consistency.

Children can feel secure in their new family structure if their expectations are consistently satisfied, such as being picked up at the same time every day after school or having both parents attend their sporting events.

By adhering to your parenting strategy, you can prevent your kids from having to reevaluate their expectations in response to unforeseen changes.

Maintaining Flexibility as a Co-parent. Co-parents will occasionally experience frustrating misunderstandings that result in misunderstandings. Being understanding of the occasional error will be crucial, as long as it does not define your co-parenting generally.

Parents will have to solicit favors from one another. Schedules shift, appointments are missed, and communications occasionally become strained.

Do not allow your communication to lapse as a result of these errors. Instead, take the initiative to reorient yourself.

Adults find these communication gaps to be very aggravating. But if parents let such chasms grow wider, it's the kids who end up paying the price.

Find a strategy to calmly get through your angry times while taking precautions to prevent similar problems from happening again in the future.

Respect is an absolute value.
Even after the sexual relationship is over, having kids keeps parents together. Respect amongst co-parents is necessary for the well-being of any family, even if they are not close friends. It should be impossible to compromise on maintaining a basic level of politeness in your communications. That decorum is essential to maintaining fruitful discussion.

You might discover that the same communication techniques you employed before your divorce are insufficient to resolve conflicts in your co-parenting partnership. Don't be upset if text messages and phone calls no longer function for you.

More conventional methods of communication can occasionally aggravate conflict rather than resolve it. Co-parenting creates a unique set of stresses.

Prioritize your children

It may seem like a no-brainer that you should put your children's needs before your own, but controlling your own emotions is frequently easier said than done while co-parenting.

Only when co-parents are earnest in their objectives and cognizant of their reasons can a team raise happy and healthy children. Otherwise, your co-parenting attempts may suffer if you become too frustrated or harbor old grudges.

While being open and honest about your emotions, remember that your child's connection with the other parent need not mirror yours.

Every co-parent should make every effort to strengthen their child's relationship with the other parent, barring major health or safety issues. When you're a child, having your parents' love and support is not "too much of a good thing."

Co-Parents Put Their Kids First

In what sense is co-parenting? Putting your children's needs and welfare first is what it means in the simplest terms. To address those requirements and create happy, healthy children entails working openly and honestly with your co-parent.

Giving children the security they need while acknowledging that life isn't perfect is what is meant by this. All parties concerned must work together and be adaptable.

The goal of co-parenting is to create kids who will remember their parents' sacrifices for their benefit fondly and with appreciation.

Chapter 2: Co-Parenting Myths You Should Be Aware Of.

Co-parenting is one issue that you will soon have to deal with if you have children and are divorced. Co-parenting with your ex-spouse may be challenging for you, depending on the specifics of your divorce. The co-parenting process may be unpleasant due to your different parenting philosophies.

The wonderful thing about co-parenting is that every situation is unique. Based on your needs and the needs of your children, you and your ex-spouse can create your parenting schedule. Take a look at the truth behind a few common myths about co-parenting that might be making you uneasy.

Myth No. 1: Your co-parent and you must get along.

One widespread myth regarding effective co-parenting is that you and your ex-spouse must remain friends after the divorce to do so. You might believe you would never be friends with your ex-spouse if you recently got divorced or if the circumstances surrounding your divorce were very stressful.

The reality is that effective co-parenting does not require friendship between you and your ex-spouse. Doing so now can be detrimental for you emotionally and intellectually.

Instead, you and your ex-spouse should focus on fostering a productive working relationship. To establish a productive working relationship, you must set up some sound boundaries. Create a communication plan first. Talk about the communication strategy that both of you find most effective.

How much, if any, of your private lives you will share should be decided by the two of you. In the beginning, you might wish to restrict these kinds of conversations. Keep all of your conversation centered on the needs of the kids.

Misconception #2: Constant Compromise Is Necessary

You could believe that to properly co-parent, you two must constantly make concessions regarding your desires for the kids. Compromise is frequently a good strategy to resolve conflicts, although it is not always possible to reach an agreement. You might not always find common ground. This does not imply that you cannot successfully co-parent.

You need to be ready to give ground on some topics at various stages in your co-parenting arrangement, especially if the issue is not a major one for you. Giving in on some matters could improve your co-parenting arrangement. Your partner will be more open to hearing your viewpoint on other crucial matters if they see that you are willing to compromise and allow your ex-spouse to win some arguments.

You might need to return to court for mediation if you can't agree on specific matters involving your kids. To find a solution for your kids is the objective. On matters you both can't agree on, mediation could be the just course of action. A healthy method to make decisions that are significant to you is through mediation, which is not a sign of a failure to communicate.

Misconception #3: A legal parenting plan won't cause you any issues.

A parenting plan that defines the obligations of each parent following divorce may be part of your custody agreement. You might still run into some problems, though. There may be gaps in the parenting schedule you create in court. In addition, the requirements of each parent or the children may alter.

You can use your parenting plan as a starting point when you and your ex-spouse disagree. If the subject you disagree on is not addressed in your parenting plan, you must either have a conversation about it together or seek legal advice. If new difficulties come up, you might need to request a revision to your parenting plan.

Chapter 3: Parenting Plan

Parents who are living apart are frequently inclined to view their time with their children as their own one-on-one time. However, you must recognize that a child's life is more complicated than that. They might contact the other parent while living with you for valid reasons that could be both personal and practical.

A Parenting Plan: What Is It?

An outline of a child's upbringing by single parents is contained in a parenting plan. A visiting schedule and guidelines for decision-making, such as who selects where a child will attend school, are important components. Parenting arrangements may be made by the parents themselves or, in the event of a dispute, finally approved by a judge.

A parenting plan is advantageous for any child whose parents will be raising them apart from one another. Everybody benefits from the assurance that a solid plan provides by outlining each parent's duties in detail. A sound strategy reduces the likelihood of upcoming conflicts.

Parenting plans might be brief, extensive, or somewhere in the middle. What is key is that the plan has enough structure to enable the parents to collaborate successfully. Let's look at how you, as a parent, may design a parenting strategy that ensures your child has a wonderful upbringing.

What Advantages Do Parenting Plans Offer?

A parenting plan, which specifies the child's expectations for custody, visitation, and parental duty, is established by the child's parents (or the court in circumstances where the parents cannot agree). This could involve anything from deciding which parent will have primary custody to more intricate issues like choices for the child's social, academic, and medical needs. The parenting plan's main goal is to make sure that the parents are acting in the child's best interests.

In the event of divorce, a parenting plan can be very advantageous to both the parents and the child. Both parents will have the opportunity to participate in determining the future needs and well-being of the child by developing a parenting plan.

The parenting plan will also aid in resolving any differences that may occur, eliminating hostility between the parents, and facilitating communication because the parents may not always agree on how to best meet the child's needs moving forward.

The parenting plan will help the youngster feel secure in the knowledge that their needs are being met. This can assist in giving the youngster more stability and assisting them in developing expectations for the future.

The best way to make a parenting plan?

A parenting plan is a written agreement that both parents agree upon, sign, and if necessary, file with the courts. As parents negotiate the separation or divorce process, a parenting plan can assist in opening channels of communication between them, minimizing conflict, and promoting stability for the child.

A parenting plan that addresses the needs of the child or children can be developed by parents working together. To form a parenting plan, they may, if required, seek the counsel of an attorney.

When the parenting plan must be submitted to the court system, working with a family lawyer may be extremely beneficial. The legal standards for what must be included in a parenting plan vary by state.

These days, creating a parenting plan online using a model or template is simple. Additionally, by providing answers to questions, you can quickly build a strategy. Plans created online can be manually modified during a negotiation process to include particular clauses or make changes.

The capability of online planners to produce an ideal custody schedule is a significant benefit. The timetable automatically takes into account details like the custody arrangement and the distance between the parents' homes and the school district.

What Else Should Go Into a Parenting Plan?

Depending on the state in which you reside, a parenting plan may need to meet different standards, but it must at the very least include:

A timetable for the other parent's visitation and agreement on who will have custody of the child (including holidays and vacations).

Decide who will be financially liable for the child's extracurricular activities, healthcare, and educational expenses

How each parent will speak to the child and how they will interact with one another as parents

A contingency plan outlining what will happen if the child is ill on the day of the visitation, there is an emergency, or there are other unanticipated events

How a disagreement will be settled if the parents are unable to agree on a solution?

Design with simplicity and usability in mind
Parenting plans should generally avoid being overly prescriptive while yet being explicit about duties and responsibilities.

It might be simpler, for instance, to completely omit birthday provisions from the plan. It can be left up to the parents to come to an informal agreement over what happens each time a child celebrates a birthday rather than establishing guidelines. If nothing else, a parent who doesn't have time on a child's birthday may just have to celebrate it the day before or the day after.

Another way to keep financial responsibilities simple is to assign specific duties to each parent, such as having the mother pay for school uniforms and the father purchase sports equipment. A good parenting plan eliminates the need for parents to monitor one other's financial activities.

Chapter 4: Co-Parenting Limits; The Rules and Guidelines.

When there are established boundaries, you might be surprised at how easy co-parenting is. I can assure you that co-parenting gets easier with time. To help everyone get there more quickly, we have created a set of rules to adhere to for peaceful and effective co-parenting.

The unwritten rule, in this case, is simplicity. Since you and your ex aren't currently dating, you don't need to be particularly polite. You all have responsibilities as parents. You can focus more on the kids in general and your parenting obligations by establishing co-parenting boundaries.

These rules are generally applicable in all situations. There may be a new relationship, a toxic or narcissistic ex, a great deal of tension, or inappropriate behavior that you must cope with. In any case, follow the rules religiously until you find a routine that works for everyone.

1. ***Start by using a custody schedule.***

Only retaining your child(ren) as long as the visiting or custody schedule is allowed, is the first boundary condition.

Co-parenting takes a plan if you want to be successful, just like anything else in life. A custody arrangement should be part of the parenting plan (often fortnightly). Some parents start with a custody arrangement and draft a parenting plan from scratch.

Each parent needs to know when it is their turn to spend time with the kids. The timetable must be followed, and both parents must be dependable and prompt with transitions. It's essential to be precise. While a few minutes here and there are acceptable, parents and children shouldn't get annoyed when people are late.

If you can, sit down with your ex and create a schedule (or modify an existing one). If your relationship is so bad that you can't sit down for a discussion, have a mediator or attorneys present during the meeting to discuss and document the schedule. Once everyone is at ease, make sure that everyone has a copy of the agreement.

2. Following the parenting plan

Respecting the parenting plan is the second guideline.

One of the most challenging aspects of parenting is when one or both parents don't follow the parenting plan. I'm assuming you have a co-parenting plan because it's an essential tool. Uncertainty, rage, and disappointment can emerge quickly when a plan is absent or not properly carried through.

It is very fair to ask for regular changes to a parenting schedule. The co-parenting arrangement might be ruined if there is a pattern of deviating from the plan. The remedy for persistently inappropriate behavior may start with mediation and end with both of you testifying in court.

When it comes to good co-parenting, especially when you have joint custody, the plan should be properly followed if there is no emergency. Agree to change the parenting plan as needed. There are times when you can make legitimate requests of your co-parent and times when they should. The default action, though, is to adhere to what was agreed to in writing.

3. Ignore a Narcissistic, Toxic, or High Conflict Ex

Having an ex has the advantage of allowing you to ignore them. Once you've made a parenting plan, you won't have to deal with them. The majority of everyday issues can be resolved with just a quick text message.

You could have to deal with accusations and turmoil if your ex isn't one of the lucky ones who have emotional maturity. However, you are under no obligation to accept it. You have the option to end the call when they start shouting, silently depart when they start bickering or stay silent.

No matter what their problem is—whether it's narcissism, another personality disorder, or just a tense relationship with you—if you never give them a chance to directly impact you, they won't be able to.

You always have the option to remain calm and not retaliate. The secret to success is understanding that miserable individuals thrive on creating other miserable people. You have the option to refuse any unpleasant interactions that your ex tries to initiate. If they genuinely pose issues for your child, child protective services, attorneys, mediators, and the court might be able to intervene on your behalf.

4. Use Professional language.

Communication should be professional, according to Rule 4. Always do this if disagreements are a problem in your co-parenting arrangement.

Avoid crossing the line and starting to criticize the other parent or using your emotions to manipulate the situation to get what you want. These types of impediments cause communication to veer off on undesirable paths.

Strong emotions might readily arise when you have children with your ex, at least momentarily. Unfortunately, some people have made the mistake of abusing their co-parents verbally and using all kinds of insults. But doing so only makes the situation worse. To avoid any issues:

Maintain a businesslike and professional tone in all of your correspondence.
As you would your boss, show your ex the same respect, restraint, and professionalism. By doing this, you can prevent oversharing and allow your emotions to control the conversation.

If this isn't possible, stick to writing or using intermediates until you've perfected the art of businesslike communication.

5. Co-parenting discussion.

You and the other parent can only converse about what is best for the child or children. Make this your guiding concept, particularly at the start of your co-parenting relationship.

In most cases, it is not possible to keep in touch with your ex straight away after your relationship has ended. This is because you two are still going through the grieving process, during which you could feel different emotions like fury, bargaining, and regret.

So, until you can accept one another and get past one another, keep all of your conversations kid-related. Talking about your days, feelings, plans, or anything else that isn't strictly about your child's or children's welfare should be avoided.

6. Whether your ex has a new partner is unimportant to you.

It's not your place to pry into your ex's personal life, including any new connections. Maintaining this border is essential. You don't need to know what they're doing because, in most cases, you have little power over the circumstance.

When a relationship ends, it's normal to want to know who your ex is seeing. Co-parenting may also be a valid justification for you to be informed of what is going on. After all, developing new relationships may have a significant impact on your child.

But in reality, you are no longer curious about your ex-romantic partner's contacts.

Likely, trying to manage their relationships will only cause problems.

In general, you should refrain from making comments, stalking on social media, enquiring about the kids, and asking your ex about private matters. If you find yourself tempted to do any of these activities, you can learn to stop thinking about your ex.

You should also keep your private conversations private. By withholding too many specifics on what, if anything, is going on in your life, you can prevent upsetting your ex.

What takes place when a new friend is damaging or abusive?
Of all, there are many situations in which it is appropriate to "mind your own business." When there is a possibility of abuse of any type or risky activities, such as drug use,

around the child, a youngster may occasionally suffer unfavorable impacts from a new relationship.

Except in cases when the child is in danger, a custody agreement cannot be broken because of a new spouse. In this case, you should contact the police or a child protection agency.

In grave circumstances, especially if you have evidence of an injury, you could start mediation or custody disputes. The objective can be to increase your share in the parenting plan or incorporate damage reduction measures. A rule might forbid parents from having overnight guests when their child is present, for example.

7. Pay close attention to your parenting.

The second guideline is to prioritize your parenting methods over the strategies employed by the other parent. When co-parenting, you can only have an impact on the things that you have the power to change; the parenting philosophy of the other parent is not one of those things.

Co-parents frequently make the error of becoming overly focused on the parenting philosophy of the other parent. Everyone has their parenting style, and it might be difficult to change it, even if you want to parent in the same way. If your co-parent is a permissive parent and you are more of a disciplinarian, for example, stick to your parenting style within reasonable bounds. Don't worry too much about what happens when your child is at the other house. Instead of trying to change what the other parent is doing, adjust a little by loosening the restrictions a little in order to avoid alienating your child.

Fortunately, kids are perceptive and can adapt their behavior to the situation. Finding a middle ground on some issues, though, can be beneficial. For instance, you might decide on the time together to make teaching your child to go to bed easier. You should also try to adjust to curfews if you have teenagers. By doing this, even though there may be some fluctuation, there is continuity among homes.

8. Refrain from Insulting the co-parent.

Watch what you say to the child of your ex-partner. Some don't fit within your restrictions. It also applies to how you discuss their mother or father with the kids.

Some parents insult their ex in front of the kids or use the kids as bargaining chips while they are negotiating with the other parent. Parental alienation is among the worst things you can do as a co-parent, both morally and in terms of the harm it does to your child's social interactions and psychological growth.

Remember that your kids are innocent in all of this, despite the possibility that you still carry unresolved feelings for your ex. By consistently praising both parents in front of the children, you can help to ensure that kids have a favorable impression of both of them. If there are any issues, speak with your ex directly rather than involving the children.

9. By default, parallel parenting

Until you can cultivate a more amicable attitude, you should always fall back on parallel parenting, which is co-parenting with little interaction between the parents. It is possible to co-parent well without ever deviating from the parallel parenting strategy.

If you can raise your kids together, commemorate birthdays together, and participate in school activities with them, that is excellent. That, however, is unlikely to work well during the first few years after a separation, or possibly ever.

When you and your ex are not close friends, parallel parenting is allowed. Here are some tips on how to go about it.

Complete shifts without pausing to call your ex. Have you recently celebrated a birthday? Let the child throw two events: one at mom and dad and one at their home.
Decide who will participate in recitals, how many football games will be attended, and other topics.
As soon as you can sit in the same room without feeling horrible about one another, continue parallel parenting. Never lose sight of the priority of your relationship with your child over that of your ex.

10. Let parents and children communicate freely

The last constraint is that you must allow parents and kids to communicate freely. When your child is old enough, you should give them access to a phone so they can contact the other parent directly rather than through you. Younger children can benefit from communication encouragement in a variety of ways, such as by borrowing your phone or using Skype, Zoom, etc.

Chapter 5: Seven Techniques for Resolving Conflict Between Co-Parents.

When two people are divorcing or separated, it can be easier said than done to resolve disputes. The friction between the parties may have been somewhat alleviated by ending the relationship, but people who have children together quickly realize the importance of maintaining a working relationship for their kids. Additionally, they could discover that disagreements from the dating phase often continue into the co-parenting phase.

Even though it may initially appear insurmountable, it is feasible to resolve co-parenting disputes amicably and raise your kids as parenting partners. Take into account these seven techniques to resolve disagreements in co-parenting.

Always put your child first.

Your child always comes first, even when this has been expressed many times before. Be ready to keep the conversation or decision-making process centered on your child and their needs before speaking with your co-parent. Before concentrating on your objectives, your objective should be to meet their requirements and come to agreements that are beneficial to them.

Leaving the past alone.

As parents, you should put your children's needs first and not worry about what you two have done in the past. Focusing on the arguments or circumstances that led to your divorce or separation could cause you to make judgments based on how you feel about those memories. Naturally, some situations may need to be taken into account for a while, such as past incidents that put your child's safety in jeopardy. These situations should be discussed with your family law and mental health professionals so they can advise you on how to proceed with your co-parenting.

Don't be scared by it.

While you should work to resolve conflicts when co-parenting, avoiding them altogether could do more harm than good. A person who is afraid of conflict may act more defensively or angrily than they typically would in a conversation. Keep your cool to avoid the tension that can cause this discussion to escalate into a full-fledged argument if you think that it is going to lead to conflict.

Clarify; Avoid Assumptions.

When in dispute with someone, it might be simple to infer the motives or justifications for their conduct. Even if you believe you know this individual quite well, wait until you are certain of all the details before drawing any conclusions. Asking questions can help you comprehend their perspectives and give you a better knowledge of how to resolve the problem and come to an understanding, which will help you overcome preconceptions or suppositions.

Give yourself time to reflect.

When faced with a challenging situation, it might be tough to know just what to say. But carefully consider your response to help you avoid a problem that is about to arise. Give yourself some time to reflect on what you want to say and how to convey it most effectively and understandably possible.

Effective communication between you and your co-parent will undoubtedly be useful in reducing problems, thus it will be crucial to be careful about the words and tone you use while speaking with your co-parent. Avoid using language just to insult or damage your co-feelings; parent's doing so will only make a quarrel worse. Additionally, pay attention to how the words you select to use sound when you speak. This holds whether you're talking to someone in person, over the phone, or even through messaging.

Wins Are Not Everything.

It's not necessary to win arguments to resolve conflicts. It involves discussing and coming to decisions in a way that not only maintains your child's best interests but also shields them from potentially damaging conflict. Give up striving to be right all the time because you might not be. Instead, make an effort to be fair and understanding.

Maintaining your child's well-being and keeping them in mind will help you accomplish your aim more quickly.

Chapter 6: Ten Fantastic bits of Advice For Co-Parenting with a Furious Ex

I considered myself and the clients I work with during their divorces, as well as the times my ex-husband has been angry when making this list.

1. Recognize your anger.

When you feel your ex is upset or acting out, call him out, whether the anger is immediate or more subtly expressed. Sometimes winning the battle of anger involves recognizing it. Lean into it, as my extremely intelligent coach frequently advises.

2. Be Amiable.

Whatever the reason for the rage, you will find it much easier to handle the situation if you can put yourself in a position to co-parent with empathy, sympathy, or even just by separating yourself from his feelings. By being kind, you not only set an example for how you want to be treated, but you also reduce his capacity for anger.

3. Don't Let the Kids Get Into It.

Do not expose the kids to his rage or a conflicted situation, whether you need to take such dramatic measures to prevent your kids from leaving with dad out of concern for their safety or just refuse to interact during exchanges. Conflict is frequently the initial cause of divorce.

4. Avoid Interaction.

Anxiety enjoys company. He probably knows exactly which buttons to press. Avoid going there. Just talk about the logistics of the kids. Always document everything. Move aside if you notice yourself reacting. People who are upset find it difficult to think clearly or engage in fruitful discourse.

5. If necessary, modify or enforce the parenting plan.

The best parenting strategy for irate parents are minimizing the two of you's contact. Depending on your parenting plan, parenting time should begin on Fridays after school or in the middle of the week after school. For summer exchanges, meet in a public place or time pick-ups to coincide with the kids' non-interactive activities. If he refuses to adhere to the parenting schedule, pursue a contempt action and engage the court to let him know you won't stand for him breaking the schedule. If your current parenting schedule encourages excessive involvement, speak with a lawyer about changing the parenting plan.

6. Refrain from living your life online.

Do not upload images of you having fun with others, going out when you are parenting, or publishing any vulnerable times for him to attack, whether you two seem to get along or things are bad between the two of you. Because of things they read online, some of my clients have monitored parenting or limited time. You are deluding yourself if you believe that it doesn't matter because you two are no longer Facebook friends and aren't following one other. There is always someone looking.

7. Avoid Making Things Worse.

By pressing the buttons we are aware he has, we can sometimes make things worse. Sometimes when we speak to children, they take it back and misunderstand it or miscommunicate it. Sometimes, the only option is to avoid the situation.

8. Respect Your Limits.

Many parenting plans written for irate parents include language requiring all communications, scheduling, and child-related problems to be handled through a third-party website. If the communication limit appears to be the main problem, he doesn't have to be there if it makes you uncomfortable, and you can alternate attending the kids' events if being together causes conflict for your children.

9. Defend your own interests.

The worst people to compromise their schedules and, more importantly, their self-worth to avoid conflict are mothers. The dispute must occasionally be faced head-on rather than avoided. Do not put up with his screaming at you. Do not let him treat you disrespectfully in front of your kids or allow his wants to take precedence over yours. Always keep in mind that kids can learn something from any circumstance. They also must have the ability to defend themselves, respect themselves, and resolve disputes in a composed and certain manner.

10. Pay attention to the kids.

Parenting is about the kids throughout and after marriage. Not about you, really. His feelings, temper outbursts, and negative reactions are unimportant while you are focused on your children. You make the most of your time with the kids while keeping in mind that nothing is more significant than your love and happiness for them.

Chapter 7:What Exactly Is Passive-Aggressive Behavior (PAB)?

Passive-aggressive behavior is frequent in situations of intensifying interpersonal conflict, such as the resentments that develop throughout a marriage, flare up when we decide to separate, and continue throughout the divorce process. Tragically, passive-aggressive behavior may persist for years, long after the divorce is final. Additionally, it most likely contributed to the divorce in the first place.

What Does Passive Aggression Look Like?
Shouldn't we be aware of what this conduct entails and why it harms parenting, divorce, and marriage?

Passive-Aggressive Behavioral definition:

the deliberate or repeated failure to complete tasks for which one is (often explicitly) responsible. Examples include procrastination, hostile jokes, stubbornness, resentment, sullenness, and these indirect forms of hostility.

In other words, it is a covert reaction to feelings of resentment or rage. When expected and where they may not seem to make sense, such emotions show themselves. For instance, a passive-aggressive ex-husband or spouse could routinely refuse to comply, act out with exaggerated animosity, or react cynically to your comments that appear unconnected.

Red Flags of Passive-Aggressive Behavior

Are you wondering if the behavior you're observing is typical or if it's just you or your ex having a rough couple of days?

Let's talk about these warning signs for recognizing P/A patterns:

- Anger and resistance to other people's demands
- Putting off tasks and making blunders on purpose to satisfy expectations from others
- An unfriendly, glum, or cynical attitude
- Concerns about being taken advantage of or undervalued frequently

Some of these actions might be particularly perplexing. They could appear innocent, but the end effect is miscommunication, not to mention a relationship in which communicating becomes more and more challenging. These tendencies may include blaming the other person, uncertainty, and forgetfulness (missing an appointment or "forgetting" to accomplish what is requested).

The last point, ambiguity, is crucial. It's a lack of clarity and an apparent discontinuity in responses that can make you wonder what you're imagining and why some responses or roadblocks appear out of the blue.

They rarely mean what they say or say what they mean when it comes to passive-aggressive people and how vague they may be. The best indicator of a passive aggressive feelings about anything is their behavior.

To help you understand, I'll give you a few examples of passive-aggressive behavior;

Co-parenting can regularly bring ex-spouses together, and exposing our children to P/A behaviors is a terrible example to set for them, as in:

For the past three months, he has been late with the support payment. You "return" the favor by mistakenly delaying his pick-up of the kids, which makes him growl and the kids anxious, rather than dealing with the problem head-on and handling the new wife on the phone.

Shouldn't we make an effort to discover healthier methods to express ourselves and, perhaps, end the conflict?

Even if it's not aware, this form of game playing? Not hip, not grown-up, and a tad passive-aggressive.

Another illustration?

The lady with whom he had the affair that caused your marriage to break up is now his wife. You "accidentally" plan the kids' dental appointments for the afternoons he has them, or you forget to reschedule a play date they were banking on. When they need to call their father, the service will occasionally be interrupted because you "accidentally" forget to pay their cell phone bills.

You are acting out in unhealthy ways that may even be on the verge of parental alienation because of your rage and hurt.

When Divorcing a Passive-Aggressive Person

Living with this type of spouse is one thing, but if you decide to divorce them, you can find yourself swiftly adrift in a tangled web of deceit, pricey legal gimmicks, and generally high friction.

"Expect the divorce process to take longer than usual and to cost more than you had budgeted spending when divorcing a passive-aggressive."

What makes that so? Here are a few passive-aggressive habits that you can engage in during a divorce to swiftly escalate the level of tension.

"[The passive aggressive] will desire mediation... but then decline to bargain for a divorce settlement. They will consent to a deal only to later reverse course. Just like in a marriage, you will invest a lot of work into resolving disputes with little to show for it but lost time and emotional strain.

Other instances? Attempts are made to undermine your authority with the children, to alienate you from friends and family, and to seek more custody than they desire to make you uncomfortable. It is a form of discipline.

So why should we be concerned about passive aggression?

Obviously, if you're the target of these unstable actions, you're in for a difficult ride. And don't you think that eventually spills over to the kids?

What if the divorce is done and we only interact with the ex-spouse when he picks up the kids or at a family gathering, but the behaviors continue to arise in arguments over visitation, child support, ongoing legal proceedings, and interference with your ability to work?

Even though they don't signify a mental disorder, passive-aggressive actions can damage relationships and make it difficult to work.

Even though it takes two to resolve a dispute, you have no control over your ex's actions, so try as you might to wish the reality of their passive-aggressive behavior away. From my own experience (and a lot of reading), I might advise you to avoid engaging and to stay as much as you can in context. Sometimes, though, it might not be possible. But keep in mind that our kids witness and sense our conflicts, and they take after both our good and bad behaviors.

Chapter 8: Three Co-Parenting Errors to Avoid When Angry

Are you frequently having the same disagreements with your ex when it comes to co-parenting?

Although a lot of co-parenting books and parenting plans concentrate on how to handle the pick-up and drop-off times for your kids, school conferences, and holiday breaks, these parenting manuals rarely discuss the underlying dynamics of what really happens beneath the surface of co-parenting conflicts both during and after divorce.

When it comes to the rage and frustration that we experience when we are having co-parenting difficulties, it is quite easy for us to place the blame for everything that goes wrong on our ex-spouse.

However, if our objective is to have a more amicable, professional, and less acrimonious relationship with our ex-spouse, we also need to consider how our actions may be stoking the embers.

The following are three co-parenting blunders to avoid when you're upset:

1. **Withholding crucial information from the other parent about the child.** To avoid having to cope with seeing your ex at your child's significant forthcoming sporting events, activities, or school performances, have you purposely avoided communicating with your child's other parent? The other parent may treat you the same way the following time if they become angry and resentful after learning that they missed their

child's event through your child or other family members.

2. **Confronting the other parent of your child in a public place.** Have your ex-spouse's emails or phone calls gone unanswered, and now you know you'll be seeing him or her in person at one of your kids' events, is this something you want to know? Even though it would be alluring to make plans to speak with them briefly in the lobby or parking lot, this rarely results in a common understanding. Catching your ex-spouse off guard frequently results in a blaming match where many accusations are shot back and forth with no real resolution, which is terrible for your children and anybody else around you.

3. **Request that your child not tell their other parent any sensitive information.** Do you intend to relocate soon but don't want to

tell your ex till the last box has been opened? Have you informed your kids not to tell their other parent that their significant other would be moving in with you soon? The other parent may find out later that you conspired with your child to leave them out if you told your children to keep such important information a secret from them, which might be a technique to control the flow of information.

Chapter 9: Eight Guidelines for Promoting a Positive Co-Parenting Relationship.

The idea of harmonious co-parenting is somewhat foreign to the majority of divorced families.
So how can a parent provide their child the finest care possible while maintaining a positive marriage? Even though part of his or her behavior disgusts you and you couldn't get along, or you wouldn't have broken up.

For instance, I have a friend whose ex frequently cheated on her with other women. He eventually got married to one of her closest friends after becoming pregnant by her. This was true even before their relationship had died. Sharing custody and laughing on Skype with her son's stepmother during the summers when he is sent halfway around the world to stay with the father, she is successfully co-parenting. I had a hard time accepting that, but I have seen it for myself.

She is not alone in this. A few of my girlfriends are peacefully and even joyfully co-parenting with their ex-spouses, and I have put together a brief list of advice I've gathered for making this co-parenting thing work using their wealth of experience (most have been divorced for more than five years)
.

1: *Pay attention to building a life that makes you happy.* Nobody else is in charge of making you happy (especially now that he's gone), and if you spend all of your precious, limited time and energy worrying about what your ex is doing, you won't have much left over for yourself. Additionally, if you are co-parenting, you and your ex are sharing at least some of the responsibility for child care.

This indicates that occasionally you have a free babysitter. Get involved in an activity that you haven't had time for while attending to family obligations full-time. Socialize. Keep reading. Dream when gazing up at the sky. anything brings you joy.

2. If you must, but only once, express how you feel about the past. Beating a dead horse is fruitless because a lot of the reasons you're apart are due to unfulfilled expectations, disappointments, and unresolved communication problems. Why do you think he'd suddenly change now if he didn't hear you when you were together?

3. Exercise. This one offers two advantages. Numerous studies have shown that moderate exercise of any form increases endorphins, induces a contemplative pause since the brain must concentrate on the body, and lowers overall stress levels regardless of the source.

Additionally, someday you'll think about a new partner or run into your ex, and feeling good about yourself is fantastic for your ego and self-esteem.

4. Keep in mind that you are doing it for the child(s). Some people stay in unhappy marriages for the rest of their lives because they believe that divorce is terrible for their children. Is that true? Recently, more research has been devoted to comparing the results of children raised in unhappy sole custody or shared custody situations against those raised in bad marriages, and the evidence points towards happiness. When the parents are content and loving, the results for the kids are excellent. Repeat to yourself, "I want peace for the sake of my child and I'm going to be gentler than I ever thought I could be," whenever you feel like ripping your ex-throat partner's out for whatever the cause may be.

5. Don't let money be the only thing a father can give that is worthwhile. After separation, a woman may find herself in a wide range of financial circumstances. Money is not the only method a father can demonstrate his love for his child, regardless of the amount, the reason it cannot be given, or the current circumstances. If you're fighting over money but can get by without the additional you're fighting over, stop arguing. All of us have our limitations, but we must make the most use of what we have. Maybe in the future things will change, maybe not... However, it would be dangerous to entirely burn the bridge down over money. Love is something that cannot be purchased with money.

6. Respect the time a father spends with a child. A youngster values all visits and phone calls, regardless of how frequently they occur. Things for adults to do in their own time. Even though you want to freak out when you see him, let the child play with his dad and smile when they are together. Being unfriendly just sets a poor example and increases the likelihood that one or both of them will cut back on contact with you since YOU make it tough for them.

7. Keep in touch with and foster your relationship with your ex-laws. Kids adore having large families. There have always been two sets of cousins, aunts, uncles, and grandparents, so just because you are no longer related does not mean that your children no longer have these ties. Particularly if you are the main caretaker and they don't frequently get to see each other. Share your photos and videos, make friends on social media if you feel comfortable doing so, don't forget to remember anniversaries, and wish everyone a happy holiday. Small children can't do it on their own, and older children need reminders of what is appropriate and kind as well as good examples. You are still family even if your relationship didn't work out.

8. Be civil at the very least if you can't be friends. Surely time will heal all wounds? No matter how miserable and awful you felt, you eventually felt better, moved on, and eventually found someone else or over it. We've all had failed relationships. This will take place eventually. Be the mature person you are now and try to be as kind as you can. It might give you the upper hand, is undoubtedly not damaging, and even leaves the door open for future friendship.

Chapter 10: How to Parent When You Hate Your Ex So Badly

Cutting the cord and moving on from a challenging Ex can be liberating—even necessary and uplifting. But what if you are unable to completely cut him out of your life? And exactly how much do you despise him? Many women are forced to co-parent with ex-husbands with whom they don't get along or especially like. It sounds like hell, but if you have your priorities straight, it doesn't have to be quite as awful as that.

Your children are important; they come first.
Even though you are aware that "it's about the children," does this help to lessen or ease your raging resentment toward your ex? For the time being, keep in mind that divorced moms just like you have faced similar

challenging situations. Consider neutral ground, organization, and boundaries. These ideas will simplify things for everyone.

For instance, decide how you will continue to speak with your ex. Set limits to help you feel safer and less threatened or receptive to his actions and words. Utilize a custody schedule

Create a timetable using a tool so that it is clear who is responsible for the kids and when. You may communicate with your ex less and keep organized by maintaining a regular schedule. Use the tool you select to keep track of various schedules for holidays, summer breaks, and more, and to make modifications. A shared file can also be a great approach to inform the other parent without speaking to them directly about key details like doctor's appointments and academic progress.

Take note of everything.

Many different types of arguments can be avoided by keeping a journal of ordinary events. Do you split the costs? To make things simple and hold each other accountable without having to speak in person, use a digital tracker. Does your ex frequently renege on the conditions of your parenting plan? If your ex doesn't abide by the court order, document each infraction. Use a digital tool with a journaling capability or keep a file.

Keep your interactions with your ex-spouse and your child apart.

Permit your child to get along well with your ex. Your child still has a right to visit him even if you don't want them to. Even if you don't like him, your child may still get along with him. Regarding visitation with you and his father, your child has rights. All of the recommendations in this post assist you in practicing self-care while looking out for your child's interests and letting them appreciate their father.

If you must, use a third party for transfers.
Want to avoid dealing with your ex each time one of you leaves the kids off? Choose a dependable third party—possibly a grandmother or friend—to pick up the children and deliver them to the other parent's house or a predetermined meeting location. You may send your child off with a smile rather than feeling scared or uncomfortable whenever it's visitation time and prevent any potential snarky remarks or arguments with your Ex.

Make use of a parenting coordinator.
Parenting coordinators, who specialize in resolving fights in high-conflict circumstances and comprehend children's demands, can assist you and your co-parent

in resolving any ongoing disagreements. A parenting coordinator will ensure that you both adhere to the parenting schedule you and your ex-spouse have established. If your ex is challenging to deal with, having someone to keep them (and you) in check could reduce your stress and enable everyone to concentrate on your child and their best interests.

Don't disparage your ex.

Not in front of him or your children, at least. Avoid exposing your children to critical remarks or arguments, even though it can be beneficial to express your feelings to a friend, therapist, or coach. Children suffer harm when their parents fight, even over seemingly little issues or remarks, according to studies.

Children can sense when you and your co-parent are arguing, so try to avoid both major arguments and minor disagreements.

Find assistance for you.

Even if you try to always take the high road, you are still a human and occasionally need to wallow in the muck. Locate a location where it is safe for you to express your true emotions. Locate a space where you may begin to heal and address all the emotions you are experiencing as a result of the divorce. You'll learn to accept your emotions and advance your healing as you start to comprehend what divorce recovery entails.

An online women's guided divorce support group may be the ideal, caring environment for you to commit to your intention and carry out the work necessary to help you get past the hatred and become the person you genuinely want to be.

Put your child first.

Your relationship with your ex now is ultimately about your child. When you begin to waver, change your direction and maintain your attention there while taking care of yourself. You should set an example for your youngster in this regard. You also desire this for yourself.

Symptoms of poor co-parenting.

Good parenting is challenging. In many ways, being a good co-parent is much more difficult. You're attempting to coordinate child-rearing activities with someone who lives in a different household, for starters. Another reason is that you might still be at odds with the person you're trying to help your child develop a good relationship with. Both of those endeavors can be challenging, especially if you believe you are doing the majority of the work. Without recognizing it, it might be simple to fall into bad ex-focused behaviors that endanger your child. How can you prevent this? The first stage is to become aware. Here are some indicators that you're a lousy co-parent and what you can do to change it.

AVOIDING CO-PARENTING WITH YOUR EX.

Co-parenting is more than just sharing custody of your child with your ex. It implies that both of you are actively involved in raising that child. However, some co-parents take steps to effectively exclude their former from parenting, turning them into a "visitor" rather than an active participant in their child's life, especially if they don't like their ex's parenting style. These methods can be overt, inadvertent, or even a little passive-aggressive, but they are never effective. See if any of these sound familiar:

omitting crucial details regarding the child's education, like parent-teacher conferences, performances, or activities

arranging for the child's activities to take place during the other parent's allocated parenting time without first getting their consent

if the other parent has a legal right to them, deny your ex access to the child's educational, medical, or religious records or providers.

Even if your ex is legally allowed to take part in decisions about your medical treatment, education, or religious upbringing, you should avoid discussing these with them.

not including the other parent's contact information when necessary or acceptable on school or medical paperwork

Not including the other parent in invitations to the child's significant events, such as birthday celebrations, banquets for sports, recitals, etc.

refusing to be accommodating when asked to adjust the parental time plan in a fair manner

Using outside childcare services when necessary during your parenting time instead of allowing the other parent to spend time with the child

Avoid talking to your ex about your child in general.

In the best-case situation, these actions may be brought on by a desire to show yourself that you are capable of handling things as a single parent. But frequently, there is a hidden desire to assert your authority and prove that you are the superior parent. Ask yourself how performing any of the aforementioned things benefits your child and how you would feel if your ex did the same to you if you catch yourself doing any of the aforementioned things. Being this exclusive with your ex is probably not the best course of action if you are honest with yourself.

SABOTAGE OF THE RELATIONSHIP BETWEEN YOUR CHILD AND THE OTHER PARENT.

It's bad enough to prevent the other parent from being completely involved in your child's life. Taking measures that harm their connection can be even worse. For starters, the child is frequently the target of these behaviors. Your child wants to love both of their parents, and if you let them believe that liking one of them makes you upset or angry, they will be under constant stress. If hurting the other parent is your aim, you might succeed, but if you choose to do any of the following, your child will suffer far more as a result:

*Speaking poorly of the other parent in your child's presence or in front of them

*Communicating negatively with the other parent nonverbally in front of your child

*Exposing your child to arguments with their other parent, whether verbally or in person
*Being intrusive or interfering with the child's time spent with the other parent as planned, for example, by making repeated, pointless phone calls.
*Making it challenging for your child to communicate with their other parent by phone, text, Skype, or FaceTime.
*Requiring the child to use a speaker phone or otherwise denying them the right to privacy when speaking with the other parent when the child is with you.
*Examining and/or censoring written correspondence between your child and the other parent, such as e-mails and messages. advising your kids not to contact, write, or text the other parent.
*Preventing your child from participating in a prearranged phone contact with the other parent.

*Not relaying phone messages from the other parent to your child.
*Instead of speaking directly, one parent will use the child to communicate with the other parent.
*Requesting the child's help in "spying" on the other parent or asking for information about them.
*Requesting that your child withhold certain things from the other parent.
*Blaming the other parent for financial challenges or talking to your child about child support or money matters.
*Leaving adult materials accessible to children, such as copies of court documents.

It is time to pose more challenging questions to yourself if you have done any or all of these things. The first is, what do you fear will occur if your child has a close bond with the other parent? It's common to worry that your relationship with your child will suffer if they are close with the other parent. Do not be misled; it is not a zero-sum game. Have faith that your child will eventually be able to comprehend that you prioritize their needs over their own. Similarly, if you undermine your child's bond with the other parent, be aware that it will sour your relationship with your child and that they will eventually figure it out.

A GOOD CO-PARENT.

It's not always simple to be a good co-parent; in fact, it's frequently difficult. Even though it might feel rewarding at the moment, being a lousy co-parent is never worthwhile. Before you do something, consider what the custody judge in your case would say if they could see or hear you. Consider more essential how your conduct will benefit your child. You might need to speak with your family law attorney about modifying the child custody arrangement if you honestly feel that it is in your child's best interests for the other parent to be less present in their life (for instance, if there is a safety concern). Call your attorney and write down your worries. If not, try to keep in mind that your child needs both of you and behave accordingly.

Chapter 11: Ten Telltale Signs of a Successful Co-Parenting Relationship

To the point where two parents can declare their co-parenting arrangement is working out well requires a lot of effort. There is still an opportunity for improvement for the majority of households. But instead of concentrating on what isn't working, figure out what is so that you may highlight the good while you seek to settle differences with your ex.

The following indications point to a positive and fruitful co-parenting partnership.

As you read them, take into account both your current strengths and your areas for growth.

Set Up Boundaries Clearly.

When you set limits and understand what you have control over—and what you don't—in regards to your children and your ex, it is much simpler to work together as co-parents. For instance, unless it is included in your custody arrangement or parenting plan, you do not influence who your ex-spouse dates or even if they introduce that person to your children.

However, you have some control over the example you're giving your children regarding how to handle disappointments and losses.

Have a Schedule in Place.

When the timetable is a reliable, defined routine rather than a tentative, "we'll see" arrangement, parenting time transitions are easier for everyone concerned.

Unless something truly extraordinary necessitates a break in the pattern, parents who have established good levels of communication may depend on the other parent to uphold commitments.

Possibility of Flexibility.

Routine is beneficial, but it's also crucial to be adaptable to one another. Being as understanding with your ex as you'd like them to be with you is a healthy strategy.

Even if you worry that the same politeness won't be extended to you, acting in the way you want to be treated by someone else can be more successful than telling them over and over again how you feel about the way things are now.

Respect each other.

This is just another indication of a positive co-parenting arrangement. Before leaving the children with a babysitter, parents who get along well and cooperate as parents would phone one another.

It's common courtesy to ask your ex if they would be willing to take the kids rather than leaving them with a sitter, whether or not you take that formal step. Some families may include this intention in their parenting plan.

***Basically, You Agree*.**

No two parents are ever going to agree on everything. However, co-parents who cooperate well for the benefit of their children have come to certain basic understandings about the most crucial matters, such as those involving their children's health, behavior, education, and spiritual upbringing.

A parenting plan that is in writing has occasionally assisted co-parents in achieving this beneficial degree of communication.

Don't manipulate others.

Parents who have a positive, healthy co-parenting relationship do not try to influence one another or decide which side their kids will support.

They understand that it's important for kids to have ties with both parents and that it's not a threat to them personally if their kids show fondness for the other parent.

Speak to each other about the changes.

Parents that have a positive co-parenting relationship try to communicate with one another before telling their kids about any last-minute changes to the schedule. A parenting plan may also contain suggestions for dealing with schedule changes, which some families find useful.

Children believe you are friendly.

In general, children of co-parents who get along well think that their parents get along. They don't always agree with one another or feel the same way about one another, but they do attempt to respect one another in front of their children. Additionally, they have mastered excellent conflict-reduction communication techniques.

Attend Events Effortlessly.

Another indication of a successful co-parenting relationship is the ability to attend school functions, sporting activities, and recitals without hesitation when the other parent is present.

These parents can practice putting their personal feelings about one another aside by choosing to prioritize their children over concerns about what "others" may think.

Recognize the Goal of Each Parent.

Healthy co-parents are also well aware of the significance of each other to their children. Although it can be challenging at times, they wouldn't have it any other way because they value their children's opportunity to get to know and spend time with the other parent. They have worked hard to get to this point.

Chapter 12: What to do if co-parenting is unsuccessful

In a perfect world, divorcing parents could put their differences aside and work together to raise their children. Major matters like schooling and house regulations are resolved after much deliberation and discussion. They encourage one another's parenting choices. Even attending activities together in harmony is possible for them.

Co-parenting options do not, regrettably, always work. In some cases, both parents are involved. They just cannot co-parent because they are either too furious or have too many philosophical differences. Unfortunately, there are also instances where one parent acts in a way that prevents co-parenting.

Let's look at a few typical co-parenting issues and how to fix them.

Common Mistakes That Affect the Success of Co-Parenting.

The following actions taken by parents can harm a co-parenting arrangement:

*Trying to exert authority over their ex's house while posing as a parent,
*Ignoring boundaries and rules to gain parental favor.
*Using the child to observe the other parent and the family.
*Acting in a way that is hurtful to the child or emotionally unhealthy.
*Causing injury to or implying danger to the other parent.
*Generating trouble or disruption at joint occasions or custody exchanges.

Even the most understanding parent is unable to co-parent with someone who is adamant about not doing so. Parallel parenting is one option. In this arrangement, without consulting the other, each parent sets their guidelines and schedules for their parenting time. Only the most pressing topics are discussed.

There may still be issues. Who, after all, has the last say on those important matters?

Possible legal action if co-parenting efforts are unsuccessful.

There are several legal choices open to parents who decide that co-parenting isn't working for them.

Every divorced couple with young children must complete a thorough parenting plan. The form includes a wide range of topics, including decisions regarding health and other important matters, holiday schedules, and the time and location of visiting exchanges. A family lawyer can be useful if the parents can't agree or if the plan no longer works. Anyone can use a lawyer's assistance to draft or change a parenting plan, whether they do it with the support of the other parent or not. The following modifications may be suggested:

>Transfers of custody take place in a neutral setting.
>Limiting parent-child communication to email or other official channels.
>Adding additional clauses to their parenting plan, which they can utilize to reach an agreement on or ask the court for things that are specific to their circumstance and not addressed elsewhere.

Parents should be aware that there are three ways to file a parenting plan. Parents can sign the document together to show their full agreement to the plan. The agreement can be signed by both parents as long as there isn't any dispute. Alternatively, one parent may finish the plan and submit it without the other parent's input or approval.

Alternatives to Child Custody

When all else fails, it might be time to speak with a divorce lawyer about modifying the child custody and visitation schedules. There are various choices available. Parents can, for instance:

- Intend to spend more time with their child.
- Enquire about supervised visitation
- Request that they are given sole authority to make decisions regarding certain matters.
- Suggest sole physical and legal custody.

www.ingramcontent.com/pod-product-compliance
Lightning Source LLC
LaVergne TN
LVHW050322160826
845677LV00014B/3512